Bonsai

for Beginners

A Beginner's Guide to Cultivating, Shaping and Looking After a Bonsai Tree Year-Round

By Jeremy Nash

© **Copyright 2019 - All rights reserved.**

The content contained within this book may not be reproduced, duplicated or transmitted without direct written permission from the author or the publisher.

Under no circumstances will any blame or legal responsibility be held against the publisher or author for any damages, reparation, or monetary loss due to the information contained within this book. Either directly or indirectly.

Legal Notice:

This book is copyright protected. This book is only for personal use. You cannot amend, distribute, sell, use, quote or paraphrase any part, or the content within this book, without the consent of the author or publisher.

Disclaimer Notice:

Please note the information contained within this document is for educational and entertainment purposes only. All effort has been executed to present accurate, up to date and reliable, complete information. No warranties of any kind are declared or implied. Readers acknowledge that the author is not engaging in the rendering of legal, financial, medical or professional advice. The content within this book has been derived from various sources. Please consult a licensed professional before attempting any techniques outlined in this book.

By reading this document, the reader agrees that under no

circumstances is the author responsible for any losses, direct or indirect, which are incurred as a result of the use of information contained within this document, including, but not limited to, —errors, omissions, or inaccuracies.

Contents

Introduction 1

Chapter 1: History of Bonsai 6

Chapter 2: Styles of Bonsai 12

    Formal Upright 14

    Informal Upright 17

    Slanting Style 18

    Cascade Style 20

    Semi-Cascade 22

Chapter 3: Indoors or Outdoors? 23

Chapter 4: Bonsai Toolbox 27

Chapter 5: Should You Grow? 31

Chapter 6: Trees 34

    Beech Trees 34

    Cedar 35

    Cherry 36

    Elm 37

    Gingko 39

    Camellia 40

    Cedar Elm 41

    Chinese Elm 42

    Dwarf Pomegranate 43

    Ficus 44

    Japanese Black Pine 45

Chapter 7: What to Search for 47

Chapter 8: How to Plant the Bonsai 52

Chapter 9: Trimming and Pruning 56

Chapter 10: Wiring 61

Chapter 11: When to Wire 68

Chapter 12: Fertilizing and Watering 73

Chapter 13: Repotting 76

Chapter 14: Caring Across the Seasons 82

Chapter 15: How to Show Your Trees 88

Chapter 16: The Remainder of the Story 92

Conclusion 96

Thank you for buying this book and I hope that you will find it useful. If you will want to share your thoughts on this book, you can do so by leaving a review on the Amazon page, it helps me out a lot.

Introduction

" Growing and shaping bonsai trees could be rather a gratifying pastime. It is a pastime; nevertheless, that demands a remarkable patience. When you take a basic sapling and shape it as you want, you are going to be awarded with a stunning art piece you can really take pride in!

The word bonsai actually implies a plant in a tray or pot; planting Bonsai, nevertheless, is a lot more than merely a plant in a pot. The objective of bonsai is to produce the appearance of terrific age and size. This is achieved by making a bonsai with sturdy roots which extend in every directions, producing a feeling of stability, a big trunk that tapers as it goes upward, a clear peak, and well-placed and well-formed branches. These features all blend to produce a cautious mix of symmetry, proportion and balance. It additionally needs to be shown in a pot that harmonizes effectively with the plant material.

Bonsai is the art of cultivating trees in a restricted space to mimic particular ecological conditions like great age, severe weathering, contorted or twisted form, or other elements. Bonsai are based upon and take ideas from nature. The concept of bonsai is to remake a few of nature's most sensational and lovely impacts on trees, which are minimized in scale.

When working with bonsai, you are starting an experience that is going to broaden your horizons in many ways.

You might discover a brand-new feeling of admiration for nature; you might begin taking a look at trees, shrubs and bushes in a different way. You are going to definitely find yourself looking around all the worst aspects of your nearby nurseries where they have the plants that the majority of folks would not look at two times. The art of bonsai is going to alter you is as unforeseeable as nature itself, yet be certain of something: Bonsai is going to change the manner in which you look at stuff.

In Japan, there is a connection to a number of the ideals which their society is based upon. Zen Buddhism - where the hobby came from, nature, man, change and elements all are linked into this one-of-a-kind technique of expression and meditation. Today, bonsai is seen as a pastime that enables a higher knowledge and being with nature and additionally a method to improve our gardens.

The pot and tree included with bonsai create a single unified unit where the texture, shape and color complement one another. Then the tree needs to be formed. It is insufficient simply to plant a tree within a pot and let nature do its thing - the outcome would appear nothing like a tree and would look extremely short-lived. Every twig and branch of a bonsai is formed or removed up until the selected image is attained. After that, the image is preserved and enhanced by a consistent routine of pruning and cutting.

Bonsai is the art of dwarfing plants or trees and establishing them into a visually enticing shape by pruning, growing and training the trees into containers based upon recommended methods.

In general, bonsai is a fantastic interest, pastime, or perhaps a profession to carry out. Even though well-known theologians have actually declared that it is, in fact, 90% art to a meager 10% of horticulture, it needs to be stated that an effective bonsai is most absolutely a horticultural work of art.

When arriving in the Western world, this pleasurable and fulfilling activity has actually never turned back, and has actually acquired a substantially diverse variety of plant material and methods.

When provided with appropriate care, bonsai could live for centuries, with treasured specimens being passed from one generation to the next, appreciated for their age, and admired as a reminder of those who have actually looked after them over the centuries. Although these bonsai are incredibly stunning - diligently looked after for many years and consisting of such a fountain of knowledge, age is not important. It is more vital that the tree creates the artistic impact intended, that it is in the correct proportion to a suitable container, and that it is in fine health.

Bonsai is a creative portrayal of a tree in nature. It is an illusion, mirrors and smoke which defy the senses. The ideal bonsai are magicians' techniques that have tricked the eye into seeing a far off location in the distant past. All of us need to aim to be the magician.

In this guide, I am going to present you to bonsai methods and how to cultivate your own bonsai masterpieces. The appeal of bonsai is that there is no conclusive "right way" to do it. I can provide pointers and techniques to create your own bonsai. Take part in the realm of bonsai and get a brand-new insight into life!

Chapter 1: History of Bonsai

The bonsai history is storied and long. Bonsai initially cropped up in China over a thousand years back on a really standard scale, called pun-sai. Pun-sai was the practice of cultivating single specimen trees in pots. These early specimens showed minimal foliage and rugged, knotted trunks that frequently appeared such as animals, birds and dragons. There are a multitude of misconceptions and legends around Chinese bonsai. The animal-like or monstrous trunks and root formations are still extremely treasured these days.

With Japan's adoption of lots of cultural hallmarks of China - bonsai was additionally taken up, introduced to Japan throughout the Kamakura period (1185 - 1333) via Zen Buddhism - which was quickly spreading through Asia at that time. The exact time is arguable, even though it is feasible that it had actually arrived in AD 1195 as there seems to be a reference to it in a Japanese scroll credited to that era.

When bonsai was presented into Japan, the art was fine-tuned to a degree not yet approached in China. Gradually, the easy trees were not simply limited to the Buddhist monks and their abbeys, yet additionally, later on, were brought in to represent the aristocracy - a sign of eminence and honor. The philosophy and ideals of bonsai were considerably altered throughout the years. For the Japanese, bonsai represents a combination of powerful ancient beliefs with the Eastern ideologies of the harmony in between man, nature and soul.

In an old Japanese scroll composed in Japan during the Kamakura era, it is translated to mean: "To value and discover enjoyment in oddly curved potted trees is to enjoy deformity."

Whether this was meant as a negative or positive declaration, it leaves us to think that growing twisted and dwarfed trees in containers was an accepted practice amongst the higher Japanese class by the Kamakura duration. By the 14th century, bonsai was certainly considered as an extremely refined art form, indicating that it must have been a recognized practice several years prior to that time.

Bonsai were placed inside for show at special times by the 'Japanese elite' and ended up being a vital part of Japanese life by being shown on specifically created shelves. These complicated plants were no more completely reserved for otside showing, even though the practices of pruning and training did not form up until later.

In the 17th and 18th centuries, the Japanese arts go to their peak and were seen extremely highly. Bonsai once again developed to a much greater refinement and understanding of nature – even though the containers utilized appeared to be a little deeper than those utilized today. The primary factor in looking after bonsai was now the elimination of all but the most vital plant parts. The decrease of everything simply to the vital elements and supreme refinement was really representative of the Japanese philosophy of the time.

During this time, bonsai additionally ended up being commonplace to the overall Japanese public - which considerably increased the need for the little trees gathered from the wild and strongly established the art form within the customs and culture of the nation.

With time, bonsai started to take on various styles, each which differed profoundly from one another. Bonsai artists slowly started introducing other culturally crucial components in their bonsai plantings like accent plants, rocks and even little buildings and individuals, which is referred to as the bon-kei art. They additionally looked at recreating mini landscapes in nature - referred to as sai-kei, that additionally investigated the varied range of creative bonsai possibilities.

Lastly, in the mid-19th century, after more than 230 years of worldwide isolation, Japan opened itself up to the remainder of the world. Word quickly spread out from travelers who went to Japan of the small trees in containers, which resembled aged, fully grown, high trees in nature. Additional exhibitions in London, Paris and Vienna in the latter part of the century - particularly the Paris World Exhibition in 1900, made the world aware of bonsai.

Because of this incredible upswing in need for bonsai, the now commonly expanding market and absence of stunted, naturally-forming plants resulted in the commercial creation of bonsai by artists via training young plants to develop to appear such as bonsai. A number of fundamental styles were embraced, and artists utilized bamboo skewers, wire and growing methods to do this - letting the art to develop even further. The Japanese learned to take advantage of the interest in this art form really rapidly - opening nurseries devoted exclusively to growing, training, and then exporting bonsai trees.

Various plants were now being utilized to accommodate global climates and to create neater foliage and better growing practices. Bonsai methods like raising trees from cuttings or seed and then grafting and styling of uncommon, various or tender material onto sturdy rootstock were additionally cultivated.

Bonsai has actually now progressed to reflect altering times and tastes - with a fantastic range of nations, conditions and cultures in which it is now practiced.

In Japan these days, bonsai are strongly regarded as a sign of their ideals and culture. The New Year is not total unless the tokonoma - the special niche in each Japanese home utilized for the display of accessories and treasured belongings - is loaded with a blossoming plum tree or apricot. Bonsai is no more reserved for the higher-class, yet is a pleasure shared by factory and executive workers alike.

The Japanese have a tendency to concentrate on utilizing native types for their bonsai - specifically pines, maples and azaleas. In other nations, nevertheless, individuals are more open to other viewpoints.

The advancement of bonsai over the past 2 centuries is genuinely remarkable. Possibly it is symbolic of how little of it the world is becoming as individuals from Europe and the U.S. and even Greenland are exploring bonsai as a pastime.

Chapter 2: Styles of Bonsai

It is essential for you to keep in mind, as a newbie, that no one bonsai style is the "appropriate" style. Bonsai is supposed to be a natural tree representation. Creating a bonsai work of art reflects how YOU see that tree. You are not learning from a master of bonsai, you are just being offered instruction on how to develop your own bonsai. What you make of it is merely within your own mind.

You ought to make every effort to make your bonsai trees appear as natural as you can. Let the tree recommend its own possibilities. In case the trunk flexes to the right, allow it to flex that way. Deal with it to make it the highlight of your bonsai. You need to listen to the tree to hear what it is saying to you. Then you are going to come up with a gorgeous production!

Bonsais ought to mimic age. You ought to try and predict the look of maturity in your tree-- simply in a miniature form. Even if your tree is reasonably young, you could groom it, so it appears as if it has been growing for several years.

2 features that offer the look of age to trees are the level of the trunk taper and the trunk caliper. The bonsai trunks (in the majority of styles) are going to be extremely broad at the base and taper really efficiently to the tree top.

There are 2 general bonsai styles: the informal or 'comic' (bunjin) and classic (koten). When it comes to the former, the tree trunk is broader at the bottom and tapers off towards the top; it is simply the reverse when it comes the 'bunjin', a style harder to master.

When you begin with a bonsai, constantly keep in mind that you are dealing with a living plant. Look thoroughly at its natural qualities and you might recognize within them an appropriate style, or styles. Typically you could train a plant into a number of styles, even if it is essentially upright such as a beech or elegantly slim such as a maple. Even if one style just truly matches a specific plant, you could still interpret this in various ways.

More than anything else, you must not attempt to teach a bonsai to grow in a fashion it is not used to. Research the natural growth patterns of your intended tree and improve the pattern nature provided it.

The 5 fundamental styles of bonsai are informal upright, formal upright, slanting (or windswept), cascade and semi-cascade. All have their own specific charm and tranquility.

Formal Upright

A tree with a style like formal upright arises when it has actually grown outdoors under ideal conditions. The most crucial needs for this style is that the trunk ought to be completely straight, naturally tapering and uniformly from top to bottom. The branches ought to be spaced out symmetrically to ensure that they are balanced when seen from any place. It is a rather challenging style to attain.

Junipers, spruces and pines are terrific to attempt to cultivate in the formal upright style.

To attain a formal upright style that works, make certain that around one-third of the trunk can be seed from the front. This could be from the bottom to the initial branch or cumulatively, as viewed through branche tracery.

Normally, the positioning of branches follows a pattern. The initial branch up from the based is the lengthiest and in proportion generally is taught to grow to around a third of the overall tree height. This is the heftiest branch, nearly making a right angle to the trunk.

The second branch precisely opposes the initial one and is higher on the trunk. When the branch structure goes up, they taper, taking a rather cone-like shape.

The bonsai top is normally really dense with foliage - so complete and firmly ramified that it is tough to see its inner structure due to the mass of needles or leaves.

The tip of this bonsai style additionally has a small curve, to lean forward and successfully 'take a look at the viewer.' Depending upon what tree species you are utilizing, the entire tree does not need to be in proportion, but rather the branches might go up by alternating on every side.

The trunk and branches of a formal upright bonsai constantly take on a really distinct taper. This is attained by slicing off the growing tip of the branch or trunk with every brand-new year and wiring a brand-new branch in place to create the apex. This is a thing rather tough to do. Nevertheless, it creates a sensational outcome when the trunk begins to develop and the taper begins ending up being prominent.

Informal Upright

In nature, trees like that bend or change their direction far from wind or shade other buildings or trees, or in the direction of the light. In an informal upright bonsai, the trunk ought to somewhat flex to the left or right - yet never towards the person. This goes for all kinds of bonsai. Neither the branches nor trunk ought to be pointing in the direction of the person when the bonsai is seen from ahead.

For this style, attempt a Trident maple, a Japanese maple or nearly any conifer and ornamental tree. You are going to have a remarkable outcome with a pomegranate or other blooming tree.

An informal upright bonsai essentially utilizes the identical principles of the formal upright bonsai with the exception of it being informal. The style still needs a tapered trunk, nevertheless the branch positioning and trunk direction is more informal and closer to how a tree would appear when subjected to the elements at an early age. The trunk generally takes on an unanticipated series of twists or a curve and the branches are hence placed to stabilize this impact.

Just like formal upright, the tree crown is generally really loaded with foliage and in spite of the informal trunk, is often situated straight above the tree base. This is a quality of the informal upright style, and if not carried out such as this, the tree would be slanting.

Jin (carved remains of dead or undesirable branches to appear like dead and decaying tree limbs) is additionally better suited and effective with the informal upright style.

Slanting Style

Trees which slant organically happen due to deep shade or buff setting winds throughout early growth. Whether curved or directly, the entire trunk leans at a precise angle. The more powerful roots develop out on the side, far from the trunk angle, to sustain the weight.

Nearly any kind of tree is going to work effectively with this style.

This style bears an excellent resemblance to the informal upright. The trunk could be either straight or curved, yet need to be on an angle to either the left or right, with the apex not straight across the bonsai base.

This style is rather an easy one that could be attained by numerous techniques. At an early age, the bonsai could be trained to an angle by wiring the trunk up until it is in place. Additionally, the tree could be pushed to grow in a slanted style by placing the real pot on a slant, inducing the tree to grow unusually.

With informal upright, formal upright and slanted styles, the number 3 is substantial.

The lowest branches are organized in 3s, and this grouping starts one-third of the path up the trunk. The lowest three branches nearly surround the trunk, with 2 branches going forward, one somewhat higher than another. The 3rd branch, emanating from a point in between the initial 2, is placed to make the foliage seem lower than the other 2.

This pattern provides a simple way to distinguish back from front and establishes the tone of the whole composition.

Cascade Style

The cascade bonsai cultivation goes beneath the container base. The trunk comes with a natural taper and provides the look of natural forces pulling versus the gravity. Branches seem to be looking for the light. The main winding trunk is similar to a stream going down the mountain side.

There are numerous kinds of trees that could be utilized to attain a cascading bonsai. The secret here is to ensure the tree isn't upright and straight naturally. You shouldn't attempt and coax an organically straight trunk tree into a cascading bonsai.

If done properly, this bonsai style could be rather visually pleasing. The trunk, which is tapered, grows down beneath the container and provides the appearance of the tree being drawn down by gravitational pull. The tree trunk typically additionally twists as if to imitate a winding stream with sophisticated alternating branches extending from it.

All that is needed to produce this style is a narrow, tall pot that is going to improve the style and accommodate the cascade and a plant species that are going to voluntarily embrace this style if trained.

The primary trunk ought to be wired to spill down and over the pot pot, with the primary aim on the significant bend (creating an upside-down U shape). The emphasis ought to additionally be kept on maintaining the branches even and horizontal to the practically directly vertical trunk. Another significant element to keep in mind is that both semi-cascade and cascade ought to be placed right into the pot middle, the reverse of what you would do for any other style.

Semi-Cascade

The semi-cascade tip, like a cascade, projects across the container rim, yet does not drop beneath its base. The style happens naturally when trees grow on overhang or cliffs. The trunk angle in this bonsai is not accurate, as long as the impact is highly horizontal, even if the plant grows well beneath the pot rim level. Any subjected roots ought to stabilize the trunk.

Blooming cherry trees, junipers and cedars function extremely well in this bonsai style. Lots of people feel this bonsai style is the embodiment of beauty.

Generally, bonsai growing is seen as an outdoor art. Considering that bonsai is a tree miniaturization and tree in a pot, one might question which is superior-- inside or outdoor bonsai gardening. The opinions differ.

Chapter 3: Indoors or Outdoors?

One side of the argument is that trees are plants for the outdoors and placing them into pots does not change them into indoor plants. Many think that if you place bonsai indoors, they are going to pass away. While not always true, you are going to most likely see far better outcomes in case you allow your bonsai thrive outdoors rather than inside.

Simply bear in mind that will be cultivating and growing a tree in a pot or tray. Trees require great deals of sunshine and care to grow. Even if the trees remain in a pot or tray rather than on the ground, that does not indicate they do not require the identical care.

Nevertheless, Bonsai are still trees and need to have outside living conditions. Trees require excellent light, excellent humidity levels, great airflow and, most importantly, lots of species REQUIRE the winter cold to go dormant. Within our homes, trees get relatively inadequate light levels and the dry air with low humidity produced by main heating systems could induce lots of issues.

There are types that are going to endure indoor conditions, and with the proper positioning and care, can flourish. There are additionally numerous species which are not durable sufficiently to endure the winter cold. Yet, these remain in the minority.

It is much more challenging to grow indoor Bonsai than the outdoor variety. Outdoor species extremely rarely perish right away when cultivated within, they can make it through for months. Nevertheless, they gradually lose their health and vitality in the unfavorable conditions they need to deal with, and end up being prone to disease and bugs up until they lastly begin to show external indications of bad-health; lose of foliage, yellowing leaves, and ultimately death.

There are numerous plants varieties which do well as an indoor bonsai like aralia, ficus, azalea, serissa, Norfolk pine, boxwood or gardenia. Keep in mind that these are all woody-stemmed plants and could have their limbs wired to guide the development.

Subtropical and tropical varieties are not able to endure temperatures beneath 40 - 50 degrees F. These plants could be left outdoors when the temperature levels remain above this. The light within your home ought to be filtered by sunshine from an east, west or south window.

There aren't any coniferous species which are able to endure interior cultivation for more than a couple of years. This is necessary to remember as a lot of effective trees are of the coniferous kind.

In moderate climates, temperate bonsai ought to stay outdoors for the entire year. In cold climates, temperate climate plants ought to be cultivated inside throughout the warm parts of the year, yet are going to require winter season protection. It is feasible to cultivate temperate climate plants inside in the winter season when they are initially provided the necessary duration of dormancy.

The urge is poweful for novices to grow their bonsai trees inside. Even though a couple of conventional bonsai species might be cultivated inside your home year-round if they are provided a dormant rest period, you ought to understand that this needs certain skills normally acquired from cultivating bonsai for a couple of years. I can confidently claim say that as a novice, you ought to start with cultivating your bonsai outside.

Okay, then, how do you begin your with your bonsai? Let's initially take a look at the tools you'll require.

Chapter 4: Bonsai Toolbox

Bonsai needs really few tools. Tools, nevertheless, make particular tasks or jobs simpler and faster. Tools can vary from a couple of dollars to a couple of hundred dollars. Similar to a lot of things, you get what you pay for. The range of quality in tools is tremendous and it is advised that you purchase the most effective fundamental tool set which you are able to pay for. You are going to come to value them with time, and, if you look after them, they are going to last you for a while.

There are 3 tools that are necessary to even start the procedure of forming a tree for bonsai.

You require a set of scissors which is going to enable you to do the quality trimming work in a little area. These scissors ought to be sharp and you ought to just utilize them for bonsai work. You might wish to try a little pair of pruning shears to begin with. Ultimately, you are going to want a set of shears created particularly for bonsai work. Potentially the most crucial tool you can have in bonsai growing is a set of concave cutters. Concave cutters enable you to chop branches off the tree, leaving a concave injury behind. The injury is going to recover much quicker than a direct cut, and are going to callous over in order to make it extremely hard to tell a cut has actually been made whatsoever. These cutters are an important component of your collection.

You are going to ultimately require a set of wire cutters, even though these will not need to be bought right away. In case you put wire on, you are going to ultimately need to take it off. These wire cutters enable you to chop the wire right up to the tree's bark, while not hurting the tree. These are necessary.

You are going to additionally wish to get a number of various wire thicknesses. Generally, anodized copper wire is suggested. It is extremely flexible up until it is bent, after which it assumes and holds its position. You are going to utilize it to place and train branches. There is more about this is the wiring part of this guide. When you end up being more competent at bonsai, there are going to be some more tools you are going to wish to include to your tool chest. These tools make particular jobs simpler and enable you to do additional things with your trees. Knob cutters are really comparable to the concave cutters, other than that they have a spherical head that enables you to chop branches while leaving little hollowed-out mark.

A folding saw is a helpful tool for chopping through branches bigger than the diameter of either knob or concave cutters. These are especially essential for dealing with larger trees.

Little scissors are excellent for dealing with truly little trees or truly twiggy development where it is tough to get bigger shears in close. These are a necessity in case you wish to perform detail work on tinier trees.

A root rake is utilized to clear the dirt away from the root ball prior to repotting. It is utilized to comb out the roots carefully and to get rid of dirt.

Lastly, a simple set of tweezers could be incredibly beneficial when it comes to bonsai grooming. Tweezers have all kinds of functions for bonsai, from pinching back brand-new growth and pruning to getting rid of unnecessary things from your bonsai. A lot of bonsai tweezers are going to have a little trowel on the end, beneficial for sowing seeds, patting down moss and lots of other ends and odds.

Chapter 5: Should You Grow?

You could begin your bonsai from seed, however, be advised, it could take a bit to see your outcomes. Unless you're beginning your bonsai pastime at age 4, having the ability to observe the fruits of your labor is most likely not going to come to fruition. While it might be lovely to be in a position to have total control over your bonsai from the start, I would not recommend it.

Seeds take a fairly long period of time to sprout and end up being an appropriate plant to utilize for bonsai - with ideally a 1/2 -1"(1-2cm) diameter trunk (unless you wish to make mini-bonsai that are around 4" high and a completely different practice). Life's too brief to stand there, observe, and wait for a tree to mature.

Trees utilized in bonsai aren't special whatsoever. They are precisely like the trees you see everywhere daily. So, basically, do not plant your bonsai from seed. Obtain a bit more immediate fulfillment by buying a young sapling from a garden center or nursery. In doing so, you'll have the ability to cultivate not just the tree, but your capabilities as a bonsai artist too!

Bonsai are common trees or plants, not special hybrid dwarfs. Little leafed varieties are most appropriate, yet basically any plant can be utilized, despite the size it grows to in the wild.

Go to your local garden shop or nursery and see if you are able to discover some low-cost plants which have reasonably dense trunks and great bonsai potential which you could develop into bonsai via training (wiring, pruning, and so on) You can even take a look around your garden to find if you have any prospective bonsai plants there which you might utilize. A purchased Bonsai is not bad. Just the tree quality determines what a talented and good plant is. Not its source.

Yet the story and experiences of a collected tree is going to include psychological and historic worth to a Bonsai that makes it boost its worth as an art piece.

Generally, choose a specimen which is going to be tolerant of the stress of being wired, chopped, and replanted. Specimens such as Lonicera, Cotoneasters and Juniperus, are recommended starters for growing Shonin. They could be discovered on nurseries in sizes appropriate for novice's work. Make certain that you purchase a tree which grows properly in your "neck of the woods." You should make certain that whatever tree you select is going to flourish well where you reside. Make certain that the plants you are looking at meet the standards for quality bonsai.

Let's take a look at certain prime species for growing bonsai.

Chapter 6: Trees

Practically any kind of shrub or tree is going to be appropriate for bonsai. Generally, a lot of specialists acknowledge that pine trees aren't helpful for the novice. When you are prepared to work on your initial tree, you ought to choose a species which is "forgiving" to the novice. Among the most typically advised is the dwarf garden juniper. They are easily offered, take pruning well, could be worked on the majority of the year, and are usually low-cost. They additionally root effectively during cutting, so you coul start your own "mini nursery" as you form your initial tree. There are certain other tree types which are favorites amongst growers of bonsai.

Beech Trees

Beech make exceptional Bonsai. There are kinds of Beech spread out across the temperate zones of the world.

They have a tendency to be cultivated in informal styles, and leaf-cutting every other year is going to decrease the leaf size on the bigger types. It is essential that leaf trimming is performed as early as feasible, as beech might not return into leaf that year in case it is left too long.

The Southern Beeches are tightly related to the Northern hemisphere beehes, varying because they have both evergreen and deciduous varieties. From a bonsai perspective, they could be dealt with as their Northern counterparts, other than the fact that you must not leaf trim the evergreen ones.

They have no unique requirements yet have a tendency to do much better in an alkaline soil instead of peat-based compost.

Cedar

There are lots of species throughout the world called 'Cedar.' Most likely the initial thing that comes to mind regarding cedars is that they come with, when inside a pot, rather fragile root systems. The roots being somewhat fleshy, are susceptible to frost damage, so the trees need to be protected if conditions call for it.

Just like all conifers, they are going to do a lot better in a grittier, more open soil than their deciduous equivalents.

Cherry

The Cherry belongs to one of the biggest families of plants in the world, the 'Rosaceous,' The Rose family is actually varied, with the Cherry family at one end, pears and apples, then Cotoneasters and Quinces, through the Blackberry/Raspberry group, past Roses and on to the Strawberries.

The Cherry family consists of Peaches, Apricots, Damsons, Plums and Gages, all of which are going to make great Bonsai. The Apricot is the earliest blooming of the group.

The Cherry family spreads quickly from seed, planted in the fall. The seeds require a cold winter to sprout. They are going to take from cuttings yet could prove hard. Plants cultivated from cutting or seed could take ten to fifteen years to flower.

They have no specific requirements, as far as their growth goes.

Pruning ought to be performed in mid-summer, giving time for following year's flower buds to cultivate.

Enabling them to set fruit might stress the tree beyond its capability to make it through.

Elm

The elm family is a group of trees which are going to forgive you nearly anything, are going to grow in a variety of soils and are simple to acquire, with species native to the majority of the Northern hemisphere.

Chinese Elm and Zelcova are the two species you are highly most likely to stumble upon on a supplier's benches. Both are exceptional trees, even though the Chinese Elm is typically not as sturdy when there is frost, however, try what grows in your location as all elms are capable of being great bonsai.

The Chinese Elm is an extremely simple tree to grow. Deciduous in temperate locations, it might maintain its leaves in subtropical and tropical regions. The Chinese elm is typically mistakenly sold as an indoor tree.

This kind of tree is one that plenty of people agree could be grown from seed. Still, be cautioned because doing this is not going to generate instant results.

They are simple to propagate. The seed germinates readily if you want to attempt growing them in this manner; nevertheless layering and cuttings are the ideal techniques to increase your stock.

Elms react effectively to leaf trimming, and on an energetic tree, this might be performed two times in a single season, yet not each year.

Gingko

Ginkgo Biloba, together with Swamp Cypress, Larch and Dawn Redwood, is a conifer which sheds its leaves over winter. Up until the 1940s, it was known just from fossilized leaves and presumed to be extinct; nevertheless, living specimens were found in China. The tree is sexual, which means that a tree is either female or male.

Ginkgo makes an excellent Bonsai, yet due to its growth patterns, it has a tendency to be tough to style, and thus ought to be enabled to take on its own form. This has a tendency to be that of the candle flame. The tree doesn't enjoy being wired and any alterations are ideally made by pruning to a bud pointing in the wanted direction.

It could be dealt with as any other bonsai, having no uncommon requirements as far as watering or feeding. It is going to, nevertheless, require winter protection as it has really fragile roots.

The soft, brand-new Ginkgo foliage could be pruned by either using tools or pinching out. Cuts made into old wood, nevertheless, are going to take a number of years to recover.

Camellia

Camellias are appreciated for their flowers that show up in profusion. When grown, these trees are most likely amongst a few of the most gorgeous bonsai. Camellias need partial protection and shade from frost. They are able to endure tough pruning during the winter or after blooming.

Camellias could be formed into Informal upright types with numerous or single trunks and Cascades in extra-large and large sizes.

Cedar Elm

Cedar elms are a fantastic choice for bonsai and like many elms, are able to make it through a fair bit of neglect. Among its positive features is its fissured, rough bark. Many specimens are gathered from the wild and are going to usually have an aged look. The branches ramify quickly with regular shoot pinching and the leaves are not too large.

This species is a great one for novices and gathering them is rather simple too.

These trees are going to succeed in practically any kind of soil. Their natural environment is somewhat dry and hot and they take well to being kept on the dry side of damp. Like many trees, they utilize more water during the spring.

They could be kept in complete sun to dappled sun. They have an intriguing if irritating habit when they are obtaining excessive sun. They are going to turn their leaves to be edge-up, in order to restrict the leaves' exposure to the rays of the sun. If they get excessive sunlight, they have a tendency to go a little yellow.

Chinese Elm

This kind of tree could be both an outdoor and indoor bonsai. Chinese elm are rather great plants to pick for novices at bonsai - with a foreseeable growth pattern and being rather flexible when pruned.

The Chinese elm bark could be rather intriguing, certain varieties with smooth bark and the others with cork-like, rough bark that cracks and ends up being deeply fissured with age - including character to the bonsai. Usually, the smoother bark varieties are going to be less sturdy than those with rough bark and care ought to be exercised.

Being rather versatile plants, they could be kept in a place of shade to full sun, yet ensure that the plant gets a bit of shade throughout the warmer months and does not dry out.

Dwarf Pomegranate

This kind of tree is ending up being incredibly prominent amongst bonsai enthusiasts. This is primarily due to its fruiting and blooming qualities.

Apart from the pomegranate's spectacular seasonal yellow-orange 'trumpet style' flowers, the dwarf pomegranate has numerous other noteworthy qualities.

It has a splendid naturally-twisting style trunk which really quickly embraces an ancient, gnarled look - something extensively looked for in bonsai. Its leaves are dark green with bronze shades and after blooming, the plant fruits, creating appealing red, spherical, golf-ball-sized pomegranates.

Fit to bonsai styles like forest, informal upright, literati, cascade, tree on rock, root over rock, windswept, twin trunk, group and twisting trunk style, this plant reacts good to hot, warm conditions, like that discovered in the Mediterranean.

Ficus

Many individuals have "phony" ficus trees in their homes. These are the bigger species. Nevertheless, a mini ficus could make a stunning bonsai addition to the bigger ones. The Ficus is a plant that is extremely fit to bonsai treatment. Figs are mainly tropical plants, growing naturally wild in the jungles of south-east Asia. Numerous hundreds of species comprise this big tree family. The small flowers are totally confined in the developing fruits, that are born in the leaf axils and are made every year. You might discover that as a bonsai, nevertheless, fruiting is not extremely prevalent. Figs choose complete sun to shade and damp, well-drained, humus-rich soil, and shelter from cool winds.

Many rainforest figs create aerial roots from the trunk and branches. Whether to leave these on or not and integrate them into the design is not an easy decision when it comes to bonsai aficionados, even though it is important for the general tree design.

The roots are fragile in the beginning, yet strengthen and become a really sturdy tree part once they get nutrients. The lovely aerial roots of the banyan fig are frequently shown in clasped-to-rock styles.

Japanese Black Pine

Japanese black pine is the embodiment of bonsai. A couple of trees could communicate the deep profundity or the power of bonsai as much as a black pine can. Black pine is a tree which takes several years to attain the fully grown appearance of an exceptional specimen bonsai. Due to this, it is necessary that those who would pick to grow them be steadfast in their uncompromising and mindful tree care. Cultivating black pine for bonsai brings a hefty responsibility to prepare and preserve great material for upcoming generations to deal with.

Black pine is a sturdy tree that reacts well to the methods utilized in the development of bonsai. Dealing with black pine is a balancing act and its development attribute is such that it requires continuous and mindful upkeep so as to remain in bonsai trim.

Left by itself, a black pine is going to cultivate leggy, long branches which emerge in whorls from a leggy trunk. The branches are going to have lollypops of foliage at the tips of the branch. As pines are typically dominant such as a lot of trees, the upper branches are going to acquire the majority of the tree's energy, leaving the lower branches less sturdy in contrast. All of these qualities oppose the bonsai aesthetic.

There are, naturally, other tree species that could work effectively with bonsai, yet this list offers you a beginning point. It is necessary that your trees have specific qualities to make a great bonsai.

Chapter 7: What to Search for

Generally, there are 5 things that you ought to search for in nursery stock.

Initially, take a look at the roots and to find out if they emit the appearance of a sturdy structure. The roots, at the trunk foundation, ought to appear to carefully spread out in a radial pattern (this is going to be less obvious on junipers) and ought to both supply a feeling of stability and welcome you to follow the tree line, concentrating your attention on the trunk. Excellent roots welcome you to analyze the tree completely!

If the roots look excellent, start to analyze the trunk. The qualities you are trying to find in the trunk depend rather on the tree style.

In nearly all cases, nevertheless, a dense base that tapers slowly and carefully to a thin apex is going to produce a great tree. In case you are considering a formal upright design, you are going to desire a really straight trunk, with minimal or no curvature.

In case you are thinking about other styles, you are going to wish to analyze how the trunk moves.

Search for a trunk which curves in intriguing or uncommon ways that has certain sense of motion, which welcomes you to analyze it even more. Follow the primary line of the trunk to its tallest point (that is probably going to be the peak). Does it suggest a design to you? Does it resemble a tree? Can you start to see the tree there?

Then take a glance at the branching pattern. While the majority of nursery stock is not going to be trained as bonsai, you ought to be searching for thinner higher branches and dense low ones. These branches are going to form the primary tree structure. Make an effort to think of how they fit with and balance out the trunk motion.

At this moment, a style ought to be suggesting itself to you. Does the tree match any specific style? What type of development and shaping are going to be needed for the tree to emerge? Do you see anything in that mass of twigs, branches, leaves or needles that others may not? How could you draw it out?

Lastly, analyze the plant to ensure it is in a good condition. Yank it out of its container and aim to see if there are white fibrous roots (an indication of health and development) around the soil perimeter. Are the leaves vibrant and dynamic? Is there brand-new development? Does the plant appear healthy?

As you experiment increasingly more, indications of health and growth are going to end up being more obvious to you. If you think the tree is not healthy, pass it on. For your initial time out, attempt to select something that is going to have the ability to endure the procedure of wiring, pruning and potting that you will carry out.

Plants picked for bonsai ought to have appealing bark, and the trunk needs to provide the maturity illusion. The trunk ought to have girth, yet need to stay in proportion to the whole tree and ought to taper slowly towards the tree top. Often, a couple of the primary branches need to be shortened to highlight the vertical trunk link and provide the trunk a balanced look.

To provide the look of age, the upper third of the root structure of a fully grown bonsai is frequently shown. All over on the tree, yet mainly from the front, the branches ought to appear balanced and seem to be drifting in space; they must not appear top-heavy or uneven. The branches must not be opposite one another with their lines going horizontally throughout the trunk. The branches provide the bonsai with dimension and determine the tree's fundamental form.

A bonsai ought to have a harmonious setup of branches without unattractive gaps. Defects could be identified by looking down on a bonsai. Upper branches must not overshadow the lower one.

Not all plants are similarly helpful as bonsai. To create a sensible illusion of a fully grown tree, all parts of the perfect bonsai - branches, trunk, leaves, twigs, flowers, fruits, roots, buds - ought to remain in ideal scale with the tree size.

Plants utilized for bonsai ought to have little leaves or leaves which ended up being little beneath bonsai culture. Plants with excessively big leaves are going to look out of proportion if selected for bonsai.

Now that you have your tree, what next? Plant it, obviously!

Chapter 8: How to Plant the Bonsai

bonsai trees are supposed to be cultivated in a container, you'll wish to pick a suitable one to cultivate the tree growth.

The bonsai, with its soil and container, are physically independent of the earth, considering that its roots are not planted in it. It is a different entity, while still being a part of nature.

A bonsai tree ought to constantly be placed off-center, for not just is asymmetry crucial to the visual impact, yet the center point is symbolically where earth and paradise meet, and absolutely nothing should inhabit this location.

The next aesthetic guideline is the triangle pattern required for expression and visual balance of the relationship shared by a universal principle (deity or life-giving energy), the tree and the artist together. Custom holds that 3 fundamental virtues are required to produce a bonsai: goodness, truth and beauty. These 3 shapes of the triangle which represent bonsai.

Given that roots need to be pruned on plants for bonsai, the preliminary containers are not the same as the conventional containers utilized later on in the plant's development. The starting containers are referred to as training pots.

Almost anything will do that can hold the hefty roots, yet it is an excellent idea to pick a thing comparable to the kind of pot the plant is going to be put in when the roots are fibrous and little.

Cascading plants ought to be trained in deep pots, while high specimens that are going to wind up in shallow pots have to start in relatively shallow containers. Ensure that the training pot drain holes are half-inch in diameter, at minimum.

Conventional bonsai pots, available from big nurseries and certain import shops, are oval, round, square, rectangle-shaped, and hexagonal. Semi-cascade and cascade bonsai styles appear great in rectangular or round pots.

You ought to position the plant in the pot middle with the branches sweeping across the sides. Upright trees ought to be put off-middle (around one third the distance from the edge) in oval or rectangular pots.

The pot has to match the tree and not be huge - generally, the pot depth ought to equal the density of the plant trunk - yet this law does not constantly need to be followed.

Select a shallow and broad pot to keep the focus on the planting itself. The broad, flat planting provides the feeling of calm peacefulness discovered in the deep forest. Discover a container whose length is around two-thirds the tree height.

In case the tree is broader than it is high, utilize the width as your measure for the pot size. Discover a planter with a width two- thirds the height of the tree and a depth of roughly 1 1/2 times the diameter of the trunk.

Utilize colors that match the tree - a brilliantly colored pot for a blooming tree or for a deciduous tree which has sensational fall leaves or more solemn and muted colors for cedar or pine. Take a look at the tree bark. In case it has a rough texture, a little bit of texture on the pot will do.

Keep in mind that no pot can last forever. Your tree is going to need repotting during the course of time to stop it from ending up being root-bound. We'll deal with re-potting in another chapter.

After the bonsai has actually been potted you are now able to include moss or other little plants around it to provide the sense of a completely sized tree.

You have your tree, along with its container, now let's take a look at how to form and prune your bonsai.

Chapter 9: Trimming and Pruning

A lot of pruning is frequently needed if beginning with a nursery plant. Just excess foliage and unwanted limbs ought to be taken out. Make all cuts above a side branch, a bud, or a primary tree fork. Get rid of all buds other than those on the trunk exterior to drive growth upward and outward. Leave stubs flush with the stems. Stay away from chopping back so far that the primary branches are diminished.

Don't shear bonsai like a hedge; the goal is to make the plant appear as a replica of a fully grown tree. Have branches growing towards open space and far from one another. Don't prune too much; plants should have ample leaves for photosynthesis.

Heavy pruning generally just occurs one time in the bonsai life. When the standard type is established, forming is performed by nipping or pinching back. This procedure manages new growth. Nipping is performed to form the plant and to establish elegant foliage. Nip off small spurs which show up on the trunk before they are sufficiently big to leave marks when taken out.

Roots need to be trimmed additionally. Attempt to maintain all fibrous roots and preserve a balance of one branch for one root if you can. Get rid of any roots that were harmed in digging. Leave surface roots unscathed. Prune the roots with sloping, sharp slices to stay away from harming them.

Pruning is essential to preserve the best bonsai shape and promote brand-new growth. Certain plants naturally react good to pruning, despite how powerful, while other plants could discover it tough to recuperate, specifically when pruned at the incorrect time of the year.

To prune properly, you need to discover the kind of plant your bonsai is and research when the ideal times are to prune new and old season growth. Usually, new growth is pruned throughout the growing season to preserve the bonsai shape, while hardwood pruning (old season growth) is carried out in mid-autumn.

One of the primary kinds of pruning for bonsai, specifically evergreen coniferous bonsai like cedars and junipers is 'finger pruning.' This entails pinching back new growth, which is at the top of the bonsai and that does not come within the basic bonsai shape.

To perform this, take the growth in between your forefinger and thumb as you hold the branch with another hand and remove it with a twisting motion. This is more desirable than using the scissors to trim the growth. Utilizing scissors leaves an abnormal appearance.

For deciduous trees like maples, cotoneaster and the Chinese elm, scissor tip pruning is ideal. As you trim outwards, trim shoots back to just after the following sequence of leaves, yet don't slice the foliage as such.

Leaf pruning (likewise referred to as defoliation) in bonsai is utilized for a number of tropical and deciduous plants like maples or ficus to decrease leaf size, get rid of undesirable leaves and speed-up growth by inducing 2 seasons of growth in one. For deciduous trees like maples, it additionally implies that their autumn nation is brighter. This is carried out in mid-summer, by chopping off 60-90% of the leaves, just leaving a handful to guarantee that the tree maintains its energy.

Get rid of the leaves with fine scissors, chopping them from straight behind the leaf. In the following couple of weeks ensure that you have the plant in a cozy climate and position and give it ample water. Keep in mind, nevertheless, that this kind of pruning is just appropriate for particular kinds of plants.

Scaffold branches are chosen quickly as the sole branches to be allowed to flourish, while the extra branches are swiftly pruned.

Take care to truly consider which branches have to go and remain so the plant could remain in balance and be enjoyable to the eye. Attempt to prune the plant into a tree-like shape - or a shape which is frequently seen in nature - to stay with the principles of bonsai.

Pruning and trimming are the ways to keep bonsai miniature. This includes the systematic removal of dynamic growth in the spring. It is necessary, nevertheless, to comprehend that for the tree health, one ought to never ever get rid of all the new growth at once. The foliage and the roots are trimmed.

You do not have to prune your bonsai daily as many individuals believe. 2 or 3 times a year suffices - normally at the beginning of spring, end of summertime and often throughout winter or late autumn.

When the plant has actually been pruned to your liking, it is time for wiring.

Chapter 10: Wiring

Wiring is a vital component of the procedure of bonsai styling and nearly all properly designed bonsai have been wired at some time in their development. Even though initially a difficult method to master, it gives the bonsai aficionado much more control of the branches and trunk of his/her bonsai.

By coiling wire around the bonsai limbs, the aficionado has the ability to flex the tree into the wanted position upon which it is held by the wire. In several weeks or months, the trunk or branch 'learns' and remains in place even after the wire is extracted.

With the utilization of wire, straight branches or trunks could be provided more practical movement. Young branches could be wired into downward or horizotal position to develop the maturity illusion. Branching or foliage could be moved to 'fill in' bare spots of the silhouette of the tree.

Without wiring, the aficionado would otherwise need to wait for shoots to grow in the preferred direction. With wiring, current growth could be adjusted there rather.

You are going to utilize the wire to form your bonsai into the shape that matches it the most. As we have actually concluded previously, decide on the bonsai shape, study the tree thoroughly and take into consideration the natural shape of the species. Notice how mature trees of the identical kind grow in their natural habitat to attain an impression of age and truth. Choose the last size and shape of your bonsai prior to beginning. Create a rough sketch of what you want to produce, and utilize it as a guide.

Aluminum wire is possibly ideal to utilize for novices. Copper wire has more holding power yet is a bit harder to maneuver. Generally, you are going to require a wire density a 1/3 that of the branch or trunk you are attempting to flex. The wire you utilize needs to be thick sufficiently to flex the branch successfully and for it to stay in place yet sufficiently thin for the wired branch to be controlled.

To make the branches versatile prior to wiring, do not water the plant the day prior to wiring it. Start at the tree base when shaping and wiring, and go upward. Anchor the wire end at the tree base by pressing it into the soil. Utilize foam pads beneath the wire to secure the branches.

The procedure of wiring and flexing results in a sequence of small fractures and splits in the layers beneath the branch bark; as the cambium layer heals and repairs this damage, the brand-new position is acquired by the branch. The quicker the branch is growing, the quicker it recovers, the quicker the wire could be removed without going back to its initial position.

Where feasible, the wire ought to be used at a 45 ° towards the branch which is to be wired. Hold the start of the wire/anchor point strongly with your left hand constantly; as you coil the wire additionally down the branch, you could additionally move the position which you secure utilizing this hand. constantly, the wire that has actually currently been applied must not have the ability to move while you keep on wiring the rest of the branch.

When the wire is in your right hand, move the wire through your first finger and thumb while making circling movement with your wrist around the branch; thoroughly work down the branch in the direction of your body.

You could either cut a wire length roughly one third longer than the branch you are wiring, or as I would advise, you could keep the wire reel in the palm of your hand and chop to length when you have gotten to the branch tip. Constantly wire from the branch bottom to the top.

The final wire turn ought to be at 90 ° in the direction of the branch to secure the wire end at the tip. On a species that is fast-growing, it could be worth wiring more loosely to decrease the danger of the wire cutting into the trunk. When wiring a whole tree, constantly begin with the trunk, wire the main branches, and after that, the secondary ones.

Bend branches gradually and progressively. Listen and look for indications of the branch splitting and breaking. If it does, then stop! The more thick the branch, the more force is going to be required to flex and vice versa. The branches of specific tree types are specifically susceptible to snapping or splitting whatever their size.

You ought to find out which tree species have branches which are more prone to snapping rather than bending and that is learned via experience. When wiring an unknown species for the initial time, test the branch tension with your finger before coiling the wire.

Certain species are essentially impossible to flex to any actual extent without the splitting of thr branches. These could just be wired when branches are extremely young and have not 'hardened off.'

If feasible, utilize your hands as a hook holding the branch exterior with your fingers, and bend and push the branch from the curve interior using your thumbs. This provides tighter control while spreading the bend force around the branch exterior where it is most probable to divide.

Flexing branches where they grow from the trunk could be dangerous; certain species could be susceptible to ripping out of the trunk totally. Proceed with caution.

Make it possible for the soil to be wired to dry out somewhat. With less water, the tree is going to be more pliable and less turgid.

Most of all, be decisive. When a branch is flexee into place, do not keep going back to it in order to move it, repeated flexing could induce an unneeded number of branch fractures, therefore damaging it.

Make sharp bends where secondary branches grow and at leaf joints; this is the place where tree branches naturally change direction. Bends create in the internodes do not appear as organic.

Include motion so that sub/secondary branches are on the bend exterior, not the interior. On deciduous species, particularly, ensure you include a motion to all straight areas of the branch. Do not simply produce motion from right to left; make certain the branch additionally moves down and up too.

If given time to recuperate with no additional work being performed, all bonsai react well to wiring. Do not wire weak or unhealthy trees as it is going to prolong healing.

Some are going to recommend that when wiring the tree trunk, the coil beginning is anchored into the soil and tree roots. This isn't always the ideal strategy as the anchorage is not good and the wire is typically going to move and disrupt the coil roots around the upper trunk. Unless the motion is definitely essential for the initial handful of trunk inches, an excellent strategy is to keep the whole wire coil over the soil level.

When is the ideal time for wiring your tree? It depends!

Chapter 11: When to Wire

With a great deal of tree species frequently utilized for bonsai and the broad variety of climates in which readers are going to be wiring, it is inconceivable to state precisely when your tree ought to be wired. There are additionally advantages and disadvantages of wiring at any specific time of the year with any specific kind of bonsai. In theory, the majority of species of tree could be wired at most times of the year, even though trees wired throughout the winter season might require frost protection in specific climates.

The only time when wiring can adversely affect the tree health to a big degree is throughout winter season, in locations where temperature levels frequently drop beneath 15 ° F. In temperatures so cold, any fractures which have actually not recovered are going to be subjected to the cold and feasible future branch dieback.

In hotter climates, the ideal time for wiring deciduous trees is just as the leaves fall in autumn.

With the branches bare it is a lot easier to wire and calibrate the branches with a total tree view. The branches ought to recover all but the biggest fractures or serious bends before the tree ends up being entirely dormant for the winter season.

Deciduous trees could be wired in spring prior to the opening of the leaves; however, exceptional care should be taken so that the brand-new flower or leaf buds are not removed. Broadleaf and deciduous trees could be wired whenever through the growing season, yet when in leaf, it is harder to study the tree structure and wiring around the leaves is harder. Branches wired at this time; especially new shoots, are going to recover really rapidly. On quick-growing species, keep checking every couple of days that the wire is not starting to dig in.

The second ideal time for wiring deciduous trees is at midsummer after the tree defoliation. Once again, with the bare branches, wiring is simple and clear; the branches ought to take to their new places prior to the end of autumn.

Coniferous species could be wired during any time of the year. Coniferous species are going to continue to recover during winter season so they could still be wired in autumn. As the wire on Coniferous species has to be on the branches for an extended time period; typically over the winter season, frost protection is required if temperature levels drop beneath 15 ° F.

Coniferous species require wiring yearly and require at least one total wiring of the whole tree for an effective design. They are ideally wired from late midsummer through to early autumn.

By late midsummer, brand-new growth is going to begin to require wiring and is going to recover quicker than during the remainder of the year. Lots of species like Pines are going to have additionally made the majority of their yearly boost in branch density by August; wiring after this time is going to enable the wire to remain on the tree up until the next year without choppinh in and damaging the bark.

Coniferous species could be wired in the spring and this growth is going to set into place reasonably rapidly yet is going to require reapplying as the year's brand-new growth shows up. Any wire still on the tree by midsummer ought to be examined frequently to stay clear of wire scarring; especially on pines that swell all of a sudden during this time.

Tropical species could be wired at essentially any part of the year since they are secured from frost and have minimal to no dormant duration. The wire can cut in quickly because of the normally dynamic growth of tropical species and it needs to be inspected really frequently.

The wire ought to be taken out after 6 months. Generally, the branch ought to then remain in that place by itself. The wire ought to be thoroughly cut from the branches. Do not relax wires as this might break the branch. Utilize your wire cutters for the ideal outcomes. If you attempt to relax, you might possibly snap a branch.

In case a branch does snap, completions could be rejoined in case they are not entirely broken. Wind a bit of garden tape around the break. In case a branch falls off, prune it back at the initial side branch.

After spending a lot of time making your bonsai look the way you desire it to, you must, naturally, look after it!

Chapter 12: Fertilizing and Watering

Watering may appear like a simple method, yet it is the second most frequent reason for Bonsai-related issues. Underwatering or enabling the compost to dry entirely is going to quickly eliminate or severely damage the majority of trees; nevertheless, overwatering can, just as similarly, lead to bad health and ultimate death from root rot and illness.

The essential guideline to keep in mind is that trees ought to be checked for their water needs every day but need to just be watered as needed. You must never ever water to a routine. This could cause continuously sodden compost, and that actually suffocates the roots.

The compost surface should be beginning to dry out in between watering. Then the tree could be completely watered once again. The time between watering can differ from 12 hours to 7 days depending upon aspects like dominating temperature levels, humidity and wind levels.

Due to limited area of a bonsai pot, bonsai care could be rather tough. The shallow containers restrict the stretch of the root system and make appropriate watering virtually impossible.

While certain species are able to deal with periods of relative dryness, others need near-constant wetness. Watering too regularly or letting the soil to stay soaked could promote root rot and fungal infections.

Sun, wind and heat exposure are able to rapidly dry a bonsai tree to the point of drought, so the soil wetness ought to be monitored every day and water should be provided copiously when required. The soil must not be enabled to end up being "bone dry," even for brief durations.

The foliage of certain plants cultivated for bonsai, as well as the typical Juniper does not show indications of damage and drying up until long after the damage is actually there, and might even show up healthy and green in spite of having a completely dead root system.

When fertilizing bonsai, you ought to do it by using a water-soluble fertilizer one or two times monthly throughout the growing season. Your option of fertilizer might differ depending upon the types you have actually selected to miniaturize.

Use fertilizer when the soil is damp and just previously and throughout active growth. A houseplant fertilizer watered down from one quarter to one half strength is going to be enough.

Another area of bonsai which has to be dealt with by the novice is repotting; a really simple method if performed properly and at the correct time. The majority of trees have to be repotted yearly or at least bi-annually in spring as the year's brand-new growth begins to show up. Trees which are not repotted are ultimately going to lose their health and vitality.

Chapter 13: Repotting

Bonsai are typically re-pruned and re-potted every couple of years. Re-potting stops them from being pot-bound and promotes the development of brand-new feeder roots enabling the tree to take in wetness more effectively. You are going to additionally have to change the soil to stop it from being stale and impeding growth.

You could tell that a bonsai requires repotting when water requires a long period of time to drain through the ground or when the roots are crowding around the sides.

To repot, cautiously raise the tree out of its present pot by tilting it to one side and attempting to move it by the trunk foundation. You could not yank too much on the trunk - so if it does not work, attempt tapping the pot using your hand to loosen up the root ball or poke a stick through the drainage holes and press the root ball out.

Afterwards, utilizing a knitting needle, chopstick, metal hook or anything comparable, get rid of any accent plants or moss and thoroughly attempt to brush and untangle the roots. Begin at the edge and slowly work around. Attempt to 'comb' and 'yank' instead of yanking at the roots - for risk of harming or tearing some really essential primary roots.

After this has actually been performed – keep on shaking and brush off the soil up until between one third and half of the initial soil has actually been extracted from the base and edge of the root ball.

It would now be an excellent step to spray the roots with water to make sure that they do not dry out and so that they do not have excessive soil on them when it is time to prune the roots.

To prune the roots, utilize extremely sharp cutters. There are commercially available scissors for pruning bonsai root, nevertheless, you might simply utilize a regular bonsai clippers pair.

In case you have actually removed the majority of loose soil the scissors are going to remain sharp, however, if they need to cut through the soil along with the roots - they are going to end up being blunt extremely rapidly and need sharpening.

Begin by chopping the old, thick brown roots which have actually come near to the pot edge and are limiting the development of the young 'feeder roots.' Eliminate a third to a half of these - making sure that you do not get rid of a lot of feeder roots while doing so.

Afterward, prune the thinner roots that hang beneath the depth of the pot by trimming them all into an appropriate shape that the pot is going to allow. This ought to be a shape which fits conveniently into the pot with a 1-2 cm area in between the edges.

The requiring portion of the repotting is now done - if you believe that you've cut a lot of feeder roots off, the tree is going to be disadvantaged, yet you most likely are going to get away with it - as new roots are going to grow from the cuts.

Clean the initial pot completely or choose a brand-new pot that is more matched to the tree and cover the drainage holes with straightforward wire mesh. As the plant is going to now be unsteady in the brand-new pot as it has nothing to anchor it-- you want to make several anchors to stop the tree from falling over due to being moved or due to the winds.

Thread a bit of wire across the drainage holes or specifically developed holes for anchoring and leave to use later. This wire does not need to be really thick.

Include a thin gravel layer to help with drainage, and after that, a soil layer. Moving the tree around, choose a standard position for it (normally off-middle and somewhat to the rear of the pot) and create a little mound that it is going to sit on. Now you can put your bonsai on the mound by carefully nestling it in and spreading its roots out equally over the topsoil.

As soon as you are pleased with the position and height of your tree (it will remain like that for 1-2 years), take the wires which you threaded and twist them together (normally with the help of pliers) over the primary tree root ball up until it is held securely (yet not too firmly) and is not going to rock. Since these wires are rather unattractive, you can get rid of them in a couple of month's time once the tree has actually settled in.

Include more soil up to the trunk base- which ought to be simply beneath the pot base. Tap the pot side using your hand to guarantee that the soil ends up being settled and that there are no spaces around the roots. Utilize your chopstick to include the roots into the soil and to ensure that they are positioned properly.

When the soil has actually been applied, you now have the choice to include additional features like moss, rocks, accent plants or gravel to improve the design. When using moss - be careful that the majority of the initial soil is cut off from the bottom prior to planting it and that the moss is not too large or dynamic for the tree or pot.

Now you ought to completely water the tree - understanding that the soil level might settle additionaly and that more soil might need to be included. Put the tree somewhere where it is not going to get extremes in temperature level (i.e. not direct sun) and where it is going to have the ability to recover. Do not fertilize now as this could burn or result in stress to the plant. You could feed in about a month when the roots have recuperated.

Keep in mind that so as to balance out the substantial pruning you have just performed on the roots, you ought to prune the bonsai branches too so that it could recuperate faster and not be disadvantaged even more. Root growth normally does equate to branch growth.

Because bonsai is basically meant to be grown outside, you need to take care of your tree with the altering seasons.

Chapter 14: Caring Across the Seasons

As the seasons shift, the bonsai grower needs to consider the circumstances and problems that may impact their plants. Due to the fact that the trees aren't in the ground, you have to do what you need to so as to guarantee that your bonsai endure the seasons.

Bonsai from forest trees need to live outside except for brief time periods when they might be brought within for viewing. These indoor durations ought to just be for 2 or 3 hours and must not take place whatsoever in summertime unless the interior is well aerated.

In the summertime, bonsai requires cool nights, bright days, and rain or mist nearly daily. In case your climate does not naturally provide these conditions, you should provide them. Stay away from any temperature extremes, light, wind and rain. Water the whole plant daily, yet do not allow them to wind up being waterlogged.

Positioning bonsai on a slatted stand in the garden is a great way to keep drainage conditions optimal. Bonsai ought to get 3 to 5 hours of straight sunshine daily, however, the site ought to be shaded in the afternoon if feasible.

During the fall, bonsai needs to be ready for the winter season. Slow the plant growth by watering less often and stopping with the application of the fertilizer. Do not cut or prune any branches following mid-August.

Winter season's drying winds and low temperatures could quickly wipe out bonsai. If the winter season temperature level drops beneath 28F, bonsai needs to be protected by a pit, greenhouse or cold frame. A cold frame is essentially a box which holds your bonsai during the winter season.

In case you place them in a cold frame, do not forget to water them while inside. Winter season watering might be just required every other day. More bonsai are wiped out by overwatering in comparison to desiccation.

In the spring, begin with new bonsai, prune the old ones, and carry on with training steps. The lingering part of the growing season is utilized for the plants' adaptation to these practices.

Generally, bonsai are fine being outdoors in temperature levels above 15F. Beneath this point, some sort of protection from freezing is required. You could bring them within, yet this might threaten the plant's health. In severe scenarios, this might be your only choice.

Simply keep in mind that woody plants need to go through a duration of cold dormancy to make it through. In case you do not provide them this time, they are going to pass away. Dormancy is a survival approach that temperate climate species have actually developed to survive during the winter season. These species have a biological rhythm which tells them to slow down the activity and prep soft tissues for the onset of freezing temperature levels. Species with well-developed dormancy requirements can not be fooled out of them. You coul have a go at putting a plastic film or tarp over your bonsai in cold temperature levels. Do this during the night and remove it throughout the day.

Some individuals promote wintering bonsai in the soil because the ground temperature level are not going to get as cold as the air over it.

Specialists feel the ideal way to achieve that is to bury the root balls, still in their pots, in the soil up to the pot rim, and to cover the pots with a dead leaf mulch. In case you reside in an area of plentiful snowfall and a fairly reliable snow cover, you might do without the mulch and depend on the snow for insulation.

Wintering bonsai in the soil has the benefit that they are going to come out of dormancy in sync with exterior conditions. That is typically not the instance with a few of the other wintering techniques, like unheated sheds or garages, cold frames dug into the soil, cold rooms in basements or window wells.

While these techniques are extremely practical-- no digging in, no digging out, no mulching-- the facilities have a tendency to heat up fast in spring, and because the resumption of growth is established exclusively by hotter temperatures, the trees are going to begin to grow and need light when outdoor conditions are not yet perfect.

No matter which approach is utilized, the root balls ought to be moistened well before the trees are placed away, and they ought to be inspected routinely-- say weekly-- to make certain that they don't dry out. If so, the trees have to be watered. Additionally, the wintering place ought to preferably remain in shade for the majority of the day, and preferred locations would be either east or north.

It is necessary to keep in mind, that the trees are not going to have the ability to endure the hotter temperature level once they have started to grow. Just as trees ended up being slowly ever more resistant to frost in fall, they are going to get gradually less resistant to frost in spring.

The closed buds, even though swollen, are going to still have the ability to make it through brief durations of moderate frosts, but once the buds have actually opened and the young ones begin unfolding, frost could result in major damage, and trees ought to be returned to frost-free shelter during threat.

Additionally, bear in mind that full-size trees shed their leaves during the winter. Your bonsai is a mini variation of a complete-size tree and it, as well, is going to shed its leaves. This is okay and ordinary. They are going to regrow!

You have actually spent a lot of time on growing your bonsai and grooming, you are going to, obviously, wish to show it off! What's the ideal method to show your trees?

Chapter 15: How to Show Your Trees

When you have wrapped up working on your tree, you are going to wish to discover a good location to show it for everyone to see. The manner in which your bonsai are shown is as crucial as their pots, the styles and kinds of the trees. The particular trick for adding to their charm by the setting they reside in is just as subtle as the whole bonsai art on its own.

Preferably, your bonsai ought to be placed so that the front faces forward and the tree is approximately at eye level. Trees must never be put straight on the ground. As your collection expands, you are going to wish to produce a some kind of display stand. You might select to show bonsai by itself on a single stand or together on a bigger bench. Most notably, you ought to make certain that the tree is placed so that it either receives the light it requires or is shielded from the sun if it needs shade.

Bear in mind that simplicity is extremely crucial in Japanese aesthetics and bonsai ought to be shown in a clutter-free environment where the plant details could be valued. This is, besides, a beauty of nature- - shrubs and trees made miniature.

Gravel beds in the garden are excellent backgrounds for bonsai, and a basic table or stand before a blank wall makes a suitable setting inside.

Try your bonsai in various places around your home - both inside and outside in case the space and weather allow that. A single display on a window ledge or the sunny area on a bookshelf might be simply the thing to provide particular rooms with elegance and an individual, lived-in touch.

Place a bamboo or redwood shelf unit in a peaceful, reflective room which supplies air and light for a grouped display of all your productions that could generate an inside-garden impact.

Turn the your home's entry hal into a formal bonsai walkthrough which offers a warm and yet extremely elegant sense to establish the tone for the entire home.

Make a deck or patio into a nature-viewing location which offers family and guests hours of enjoyment and peaceful peacefulness. Benches, railings and plant stands could be utilized to display your works of art.

Show the bonsai on all kinds of focal points or stands. The identical guidelines that apply to pot textures, colors and materials additionally apply to feasible plant stands' wood, stone, metal and any mix might work in various settings and with the appropriate bonsai.

Keep in mind that bonsai is a creation of the artist and the declaration you pick to make it distinctively your own just as with clay or paint or any creative medium. Change your bonsai positions frequently to alter the feel and look of the area they inhabit.

There are a couple of extra points to remember when cultivating bonsai.

Chapter 16: The Remainder of the Story

Bonsai isn't about perfection. It is an art of scope and individual choice. You are going to mess up. This is fine and it happens even to bonsai masters.

You are going to destroy trees. This is an unfortunate reality of the activity, particularly as you start. You are handling living things, and you need to be considerate of that. Devote yourself to comprehend why every tree passes away and what could be done to stop it. Learn from your errors and do your finest to avoid them down the road.

Possibly most significantly, comprehend that when you place a tree in a pot, you are devoting yourself to the tree care. You can not just overlook it, or it is going to pass away. Bonsai is a responsibility along with a pastime. If you practice it with persistence and care, the benefits are incredible.

Practically nothing in bonsai is instant. Expect your trees to grow over years, even decades. It might be 10 years or more before your plant is going to, in fact, be a real bonsai. Do not be dissuaded by this. Think of it as part of the process.

Do not fiddle! The temptation for novices is to constantly fiddle with their tree(s), chopping bits off occasionally, constantly misting, watering, moving them around, and so on. Checking daily for health issues and water needs is needed. Otherwise, leave the tree to grow and just take pleasure in looking at it!

Pruning back to shape is required, however, do not constantly leap onto each leaf that is not in place. So as to keep the tree healthy and dynamic, it has to be able to grow with ease at times.

It is additionally crucial to bear in mind that timing is extremely crucial, do not perform tasks such as repotting or significant restyling at the incorrect time of the year as this could cause bad health in the tree and absence of vitality. A tree repotted at the incorrect time of year, for example, might stay alive if you are fortunate, it might even grow a bit, yet, it will really rarely award you with vitality.

It is especially crucial not to stress the tree by performing numerous operations simultaneously. Allow the tree to rest in between, for instance, replanting and wiring. Just as people require time to recover from surgery, a bonsai tree requires the identical treatment.

Plants are alive, and they require complete healing from one operation, prior to the next action. A guideline is to wait one to three months after transplanting before you begin working on the tree or up until you see clear indications of dynamic growth.

Even though bonsai is a really fragile and accurate pastime in lots of aspects. Normally, the plants are extremely flexible - so do not be scared to prune. Likewise, make sure not to leave the wire on too long so that it cuts into the bark.

Discard any ideas that bonsai is too tough to understand, too pricey or too lengthy. It's none of those. Actually, it's enjoyable, relaxing and gorgeous. Keep in mind that bonsai is art - one that utilizes living plants as its raw component.

In general, bonsai trees are rather individualized and there are no rigorous guidelines to follow if you undertake it simply as a pastime which to gain pleasure out of. It does not need to be a pricey dedication, yet it is a dedication that needs an excellent quantity of patience, time, capability and endurance.

Even though things might not constantly go as you want, do not quit. Bear in mind that the Japanese bonsai masters were novices as well and they have undoubtedly had their share of mistakes.

Conclusion

Although the art of bonsai could be extremely challenging to beginners when they initially begin, actually, it is as easy as you make it. There are numerous varieties and species of trees available to grow; lots of new methods that could be found out to improve bonsai look and an apparently unfathomable amount of do's and do n'ts. An essential thing that a novice should focus on is finding out how to merely keep your tree shape and keep it alive.

Learn to care for your initial tree effectively and your self-confidence grows sufficiently to broaden your horizons and effectively learn more innovative methods like reselling and making bonsai. Yet do not run before you walk. The initial central guideline to find out when starting this art is that you are handling something ever-changing and living; the fundamental guidelines of cultivation have to be learned before you can effectively sustain your tree.

There are numerous bonsai methods available for the bonsai aficionado to utilize to reach the supreme objective of a stunning tree. Confusingly, information offered in the many bonsai books and websites could typically be contradictory. It needs to be comprehended that for each goal, like repotting, styling or pruning, there are 100 various methods or viewpoints.

Some of them are based upon horticultural truths, several are based upon horticultural misconceptions and certain ones are based upon horticultural luck! Actually, a number of these methods are going to work to one degree or another. Sadly, some advice and/or methods can lead to lessened vitality as your trees cope under stress. Sound guidance based upon simple horticultural truths can just enhance the health, look and vitality of your tree. It is for you to discover which methods work your tree and you in any given circumstance.

Simply do not get in a rush. Rome wasn't built in a day. Bonsai isn't cultivated in a short amount of time as well. Bonsai definitely requires some time, yet the benefits are excellent. Once it grows and is formed to your preference, you are going to have shaped a thing that is your own. It is going to be a thing to be happy with-- a thing to show-- a thing to take credit for.

In the film "The Karate Kid," Mr. Miyagi would say to Daniel that he ought to have patience while getting to know the fine points of karate. Miyagi showed this principle best with his bonsai. He spent 5 years growing one tree-- the supreme display of patience. As a starting bonsai artist, this ought to be your cardinal guideline. Have patience and allow nature to do its magic.

Some individuals believe they are simply not capable of growing a first-rate bonsai. That's alright, you do not need to! However, if you grow a bonsai tree which is lovely to you, you could eventually be rewarded if another person sees the identical beauty as you!

Do not get irritated; do not feel you need to be held to unfaltering standards. Simply grow your tree, spend time creating your work of art, and take pleasure in the outcomes-- together with everybody else!

I hope that you enjoyed reading through this book and that you have found it useful. If you want to share your thoughts on this book, you can do so by leaving a review on the Amazon page. Have a great rest of the day.

Printed in Great Britain
by Amazon